DEAR COACH

Real emails from parents behaving badly on the field, at home, and behind their computer screens.

MATT LISLE

Dear Coach: Real Emails From Parents Behaving Badly On The Field, At Home, And Behind Their Computer Screens by Matt Lisle
Published by Kindle Direct Publishing

www.CoachLisle.com

Cover Design, Illustrations, and Layout: Wes Molebash
Editor: Justin McRoberts

Paperback ISBN: 9781098694609

For my Dad.
You're the best Coach I've ever known.
Thank you.

INTRODUCTION

To: CoachLisle@CoachLisle.om
From: holdmycalls@yawhew.com
Subject: Are You Seriously Calling Me Right Now?

Dear Coach Lisle,

I am a 14U Boys Soccer Coach. Last season I rotated a kid out of the game and he sulked heavily off the field. A minute later, he's standing next to me with his phone in his hand. He told me that his mom wanted to talk to me about why he wasn't currently playing! When I looked up, I saw his mom on the other sideline yelling into her phone! I could actually hear her screaming; not on the phone, but across the field!

I took his phone, hung it up, and tossed it into his bag. Let's just say I had to have a long talk with mom afterwards.

Sincerely,
Hold My Calls

To: DearCoach@CoachLisle.com
From: jor-el@fortressofsolitude.org
Subject: Faster Than A Speeding Bullet!

Coach's Note: Franky is a 13-year-old we had just added to our roster. The day after tryouts, I received this email from his dad.

Dear Coach,

I just want to make sure you know that Franky is a utility player, but he primarily plays catcher, pitcher, and middle infield. He has an amazing arm and he's a natural switch hitter. He is left eye dominant, throws righty, shoots archery righty, and shoots his pistol and rifle lefty. He's pretty strange about that stuff, but he is really good at everything he does.

He threw out 15- and 16-year-olds stealing second as a catcher during the last tournament. He typically drives balls to the right when batting right, and to the left when batting left (but he's not late on the ball). More power hitting lefty, but more experience batting right.

He's very limber. Sort of double jointed. He can do splits like a girl. He's also an incredible pole vaulter due to his strength vs. his size; about average to above average in height for a 13-year-old.

We are comfortable with him playing any position as he typically outperforms his teammates.

Sincerely,
Father of Superman

To: CoachLisle@CoachLisle.com
From: notimpressed@yawhew.com
Subject: Drunk Dad Used To Have Game

Dear Coach Lisle,

Earlier this year, a father was visibly intoxicated at our 10-year-old tackle football league game. He was screaming at play calling. He was yelling at the refs. Berating everyone. Finally, the ref told him to calm down or he will be asked to leave the property.

The guy yelled "I own this place. When I played here, I broke records. All records!"

The ref said, "And now what do you do for a living?"

The Dad quieted down and walked away.

I'm guessing that Dad wasn't an NFL player. :)

Sincerely,
Not Impressed

To: DearCoach@CoachLisle.com
From: embarrassedmama@ohnoyoudidnt.net
Subject: Please Explain!

Dear Coach,

Will one of you please explain to me why my daughter will not be on varsity this year? She has been on varsity since her freshman year. She stated that you told her she would get more playing time on JV.

I do understand that she may not be one of the best players on your team, but I do not agree with you crushing her spirit. She has played select ball since her 6th grade year, and I know some of those girls have not had near the experience she has. Both of you coaches have no clue what she is and isn't capable of as you have not played a "game" yet.

She WILL NOT be a catcher on JV as this is not the position she is comfortable with. She only catches for her travel ball coach as a favor to her. I feel that you are doing this to her because you need a catcher on JV. If you do not have a place for her she will go do other things. This is embarrassing to her and actually to me as a parent. Also, if she is going to be on varsity and a bench warmer that will not work either.

I have an issue with the way you have broken my child's heart. I know she is fat, but I dare you to find another student that is as committed and hardworking as she is.

Sincerely,
Indirectly Embarrassed Mom

To: CoachLisle@CoachLisle.com
From: coach@somejuniorcollege.edu
Subject: Superiorty Complex

Dear Coach Lisle,

I am a junior college softball coach and I wanted to share this story and email.

At our regional tournament banquet, all of the region's top players are voted on by the coaches and are given their awards (coaches cannot vote for their own players).

After the tournament, a parent sent this email to every coach in the region:

Dear Coaches,

I cannot believe you did not pick my daughter to be on the 1st team all region team! Alexa and Carlee are half the players that my daughter is. You all must be blind to give them the award over my daughter who was clearly better. Our team was ranked higher and her stats were better! This is sinful! Can you all really tell me Alexa — who is on the worst team in the region — deserved this over my daughter? NO! You guys should all be ashamed of yourselves for your choices! I don't know how you all can be considered head coaches for a college program. Anyone with two good eyes could have picked my daughter over the other two rec ball kids.

Sincerely,
Dad With The Better Daughter

Coach's Note: Her stats were "better" overall, but against our region's opponents they were not and she had 17 errors (10 more than the other two girls he mentioned). Not one of the seven coaches replied, so the father decided to email them all again upset that they hadn't responded.

To: DearCoach@CoachLisle.com
From: coachwife@yawhew.com
Subject: When Players And Parents Collide

Dear Coach Lisle,

My husband was President of the local Babe Ruth League. We hosted the 16-18u state tournament one year.

A player was thrown out at first base. As he walked back across the field to the third base dugout, he bumped into the pitcher (appeared intentional). A dad from the field team was irate and ran down the grandstand to the backstop and was yelling through the fence. The umpire told him to stop, he would take care of it.

The umpire ejected the offending player, but the player didn't leave the dugout immediately. The dad started yelling again. The umpire told the player he had to leave.

The player then went to the grandstand. Dad starts yelling at the umpire through the fence again. The ejected player's coach came over to the fence and was yelling back at the dad. Next thing you know there's a brawl in the stands including the ejected player, his coach, several teammates, the dad, and other fans. Luckily the team in the field just stayed there.

I called the police from the score booth while my husband was trying to tell everybody to stop and sit down over the sound system. By the time the police arrived it was over, and the umps called the game because the one team left the field. The team in the field won by forfeit.

The offending kid's team ended up being disqualified from the tournament since several of them left the field and joined the fight, and the coach was banned from coaching in Babe Ruth.

Sincerely,
Frazzled Coach's Wife

COACH LISLE'S COMMENTARY

WHEN I AM DEALING WITH A PARENT WHO IS BEING RUDE AND LOUD TOWARDS UMPIRES, PARENTS, OR EVEN THE SNACK SHACK KID FOR DELIVERING NACHOS WITH COLD CHEESE...

Sorry.

SNACK SHACK

I'LL QUIETLY TAKE THEM ASIDE, LISTEN, SPEAK SOFTLY, AND DE-ESCALATE THE SITUATION.

ONCE THINGS HAVE COOLED DOWN, I'LL TRY TO OFFER SOLUTIONS TO HELP THE PARENT FEEL LIKE I HEARD THEM.

HOW NOT TO BE A JERK AT YOUR KID'S BALL GAMES

THIS ENTIRE SITUATION, IF HANDLED CORRECTLY, COULD HAVE BEEN AVOIDED. THE UMPIRE DOES THE RIGHT THING BY ASKING FOR THE PLAYER'S COACH TO HELP DEAL WITH THE PLAYER AND HIS DAD.

UNFORTUNATELY, THE COACH THROWS FUEL ON THE FIRE AND ALL HELL BREAKS LOOSE.

To: CoachLisle@CoachLisle.com
From: eyeroll@yawhew.com
Subject: A Failure To Communicate

Dear Coach Lisle,

A parent emailed and asked me to send him a text message every day after practice with how his son (a ninth grader) did at practice and what he needed to work on. Apparently his son didn't like to communicate that to him when he got home. In the same email, he also requested that his 'very gifted' son never be paired up with bad players on the team because his child was going to play in college and the other players on the team likely weren't.

Sincerely,
Rolling My Eyes

COACH LISLE'S COMMENTARY

I'M GUESSING THE SON IN THIS SCENARIO DOESN'T LIKE COMING HOME FROM PRACTICE AND IMMEDIATELY DEBRIEFING WITH DAD.

SOMETIMES KIDS NEED SPACE AND TIME AFTER SCHOOL OR PRACTICE OR A GAME BEFORE THEY WANT TO TALK ABOUT IT.

I'D LIKE TO SEE DAD GIVE HIS SON SOME SPACE AFTER PRACTICE, AND/OR ASK WHY TALKING AFTER PRACTICE IS SO HARD.

HE MIGHT DISCOVER ANOTHER REASON (THAT'S WHAT GOOD PARENTS DO!).

AS FOR THE SECOND PART OF THE EMAIL, I'D SUGGEST THAT PLAYING WITH LESS TALENTED TEAMMATES PROVIDES AN OPPORTUNITY TO BECOME A GREAT TEAMMATE. GREAT PLAYERS HELP OTHER PLAYERS GET BETTER. THIS ISN'T AN OBSTACLE; IT'S AN OPPORTUNITY!

To: CoachLisle@CoachLisle.com
From: didthatjusthappen@yawhew.com
Subject: Never Steal A Grounder

Dear Coach Lisle,

I wanted to share this funny story of what happened at our last tee-ball game and thought you'd enjoy.

My six-year-old daughter has a female coach for their baseball team who also has a daughter on the team. During our game last week, she got upset that another player took a ground ball that her daughter should have gotten. She ran out of the dugout, took a ball out of another players glove, and proceeded to put it down on the ground so her daughter could make the play. There was an audible "gasp" from all the parents on both sides.

Sincerely,
Still Shaking My Head

To: CoachLisle@CoachLisle.com
From: meancoach@cityrecball.gov
Subject: I'm Their Coach, Not Their Parent

Dear Coach Lisle,

Last season, I had a parent call me because she was concerned about the hours her daughter was playing video games at home. When I asked her what she wanted me to do about it, she told me she wanted me to talk to her daughter at the next lesson about how she should be practicing her pitching and not sitting in front of a screen. When I asked her why I needed to be the one to tell her that, she responded with, "Because I don't want her to think I'm a mean parent".

Sincerely,
Mean Coach

Dear Coach Lisle,

I once had a parent request a meeting with me and her high school son (he was a junior). I could tell she was upset about playing time. Her son wasn't one of our better players but he was a good kid. So I agreed to the meeting.

When the meeting started I asked the athlete what his goals were for the season and life after high school. He proudly stated that he was interested in computer science and programming for video games. His mother angrily swung her head at him and said, "Computer science?! Oh, hell no! What about our plans for the major leagues?!" The student got embarrassed and said, "Well, I need a back up plan, Mom." She replied, "Not when you're as great of a player as you!"

You can guess how the rest of the meeting went...

Sincerely,
Coach Bubble Burster

To: CoachLisle@CoachLisle.com
From: rollin_on_dubs@freshcoachlife.org
Subject: Never Help Players Be Leaders

Dear Coach Lisle,

A parent emailed me once and told me she had heard that I had asked her freshman son to coach the other kids in practice (I only had one assistant and her son was a very good leader and understood the drills well). She went on to explain that coaching wasn't her son's job, it was my job. And if I wanted to keep getting paid, I needed to start working for my paycheck (I make $500 a year as a freshmen high school baseball coach).

Sincerely,
Coach 1%

LIVIN' THAT HIGH SCHOOL BASEBALL COACH LIFE!

To: CoachLisle@CoachLisle.com
From: whycantwegetalong@yawhew.com
Subject: The Bully Doesn't Fall Far From The Tree

Dear Coach Lisle,

I once emailed a parent about her child teasing another player on the team and that it was an ongoing issue. I explained that I had talked to her about it, but she still was doing it and I would have to start taking away her playing time.

The parent emailed back that night and said, "That's just a normal part of growing up for girls. Every child does it."

Sincerely,
Parents Are Worse Than The Kids

COACH LISLE'S COMMENTARY

WHILE MOST THE EMAILS IN THIS BOOK ARE AT LEAST A LITTLE BIT HUMOROUS, THIS ONE MAKES ME SAD.

IF I RECEIVED THIS EMAIL, MY FIRST THOUGHT WOULD PROBABLY BE SOMETHING LIKE "I SEE WHERE SHE GETS IT FROM."

AFTER THAT, I'D THINK THE COACH HAS A RESPONSIBILITY TO PROTECT OTHER TEAM MEMBERS AND THE TEAM CULTURE AS A WHOLE.

To: CoachLisle@CoachLisle.com
From: packalunch@forreal.org
Subject: Would You Like Fries With That?

Dear Coach Lisle,

My high school team had an away game three hours away, so I told the players and parents the previous day to pack a lunch.

An hour before leaving, one of my players let me know he forgot to bring his lunch. I called his mom to see if she could bring something to the school before we left. Her response? She asked if the bus could just drive through and pick her son up some chicken strips on the way to the game.

Sincerely,
Fast Food Coach

To: CoachLisle@CoachLisle.com
From: toomuchattitude@foronefamily.net
Subject: Who's Worse? The Player Or The Parent?

Dear Coach Lisle,

Last month, we offered a tryout to a girl who was interested in our program. She had bounced around from a few other teams but we decided to give her a try. We had her practice and play with us for a week. She had a pretty bad attitude on top of not being a very good player and I was leaning towards telling her mom I didn't think she was a good fit.

After the week passed, her mother came up to me and said, "Thanks for the tryout week. Now, if you can get rid of these six players (she wrote a list) we can make a good team".

Needless to say, she didn't make the team.

Sincerely,
I Don't Have Time For This

To: DearCoach@CoachLisle.com
From: ifthereisaline@icrossedit.net
Subject: RE: Your Wife

Dear Coach,

I would really appreciate it if you would tell your fat, ugly, disgusting wife to stop posting annoying things on Facebook about parenting and coaching. I am hoping she can use that energy to get some of her missing teeth replaced. Or maybe exercise a little to lose a few chins or maybe even her belly. I don't wish bad on you, because waking up next to her is enough punishment for any man.

Sincerely,
A Tactless Parent

To: CoachLisle@CoachLisle.com
From: coach@whatamisupposedtodowiththis.net
Subject: You're Tearing Me Apart, Coach!

Coach Lisle,

Please note this was sent to us anonymously but we knew exactly whose parent sent it. Unfortunately, over the course of the season, other parents and coaches received similar "anonymous" emails from this dad. My heart breaks for this parent's child because he is actually a great kid.

Dear Coach,

How about being fair. My son sat for two innings in a game where crybaby Bobby didn't sit out. You tell the boys that everyone sits, but it's not so. I don't think lying to the boys sets a good example for them. I hear that's why Chris (another kid on the team) quit. He got tired of your self righteous crap. You are a poor role model for the boys and need to improve yourself. The boys are not the problem, you are. Bobby's performance on the mound was disgraceful the way he carried himself. Quit kissing his butt and put him where he belongs. No other boys get by with what he does, and Marcus played as well at shortstop as Bobby pitched. He is easily replaceable. You are tearing this team apart by not being fair.

Sincerely,
Anonymous Parent

Coach's Note: Keep in mind these kids are 9-10 years old.

To: CoachLisle@CoachLisle.com
From: coach@iwillpullwhoeveriwant.net
Subject: To Pull Or Not To Pull

Dear Coach Lisle,

During my youth football coaching years the league had a "pull card." Prior to the game, you'd select five of your best players to sit out if your team were to go up by sixteen or more points.

One game, our team went up by sixteen in the third quarter and our pull card kids came off the field. Suddenly I heard a voice on the fence that sounded unhappy. Eventually I realized this person was yelling directly at me. As I walked up or down the sideline, the voice followed me wanting to know why his kid was not in the game. At the end of the third quarter, I walked over to explain to him that it was a good thing to be on the pull card. I also explained that — at this young level — it helps with sportsmanship. He promptly told me his kid was too good to sit for any reason and to never have him on the pull card again.

Sincerely,
Parents Just Don't Understand

To: CoachLisle@CoachLisle.com
From: coach@isalsoacounselor.com
Subject: Love Hurts

Dear Coach Lisle,

Below is an email I received from a parent I'd never met (and still haven't, actually). I received it last year, the morning after we cut her freshman son at tryouts.

Dear Coach,

I want you to know that we are very disappointed with your decision to cut Timmy. This kid cried all night. He is now devastated. This is the kind of thing that ruins a kid. This is all he talked about for months. He just wants to be a part of the team. He is a freshman. I'm not sure what to expect. He feels like you picked kids based on the good ole boys. I sure hope not. This kid has excellent grades and excellent attendance. I sure hope your decision doesn't send him into deep depression.

Sincerely,
Timmy's Mom

COACH LISLE'S COMMENTARY

IF I WERE THE DAD IN THIS SITUATION AND MY SON TOLD ME HE "JUST WANTS TO BE A PART OF THE TEAM", I'D HAVE HIM APPROACH THE COACH IN PERSON AND TELL HIM THAT. HE MIGHT NOT BE ON THE ROSTER BUT HE COULD CONTRIBUTE SOME OTHER WAY. MAYBE AS A TEAM MANAGER?

I MIGHT EVEN SUGGEST THAT HE COULD HELP WITH DRILLS OR PRACTICE. I DON'T KNOW TOO MANY COACHES WHO WOULD TURN DOWN AN OFFER LIKE THAT. THEN, IN THE SAD CASE IN WHICH A PLAYER QUITS OR GETS HURT, MY HELPFUL, COMMITTED TEAM-PLAYER SON WOULD BE FRONT OF MIND TO FILL IN.

IF I WERE THE COACH IN THIS SITUATION, I'D EMAIL THIS PARENT BACK AND EMPATHIZE WITH HER SON'S DISAPPOINTMENT, MAYBE OFFERING HIM A POSITION THAT WOULD MAKE HIM FEEL PART OF THE TEAM.

THERE ARE MANY WAYS TO BE A TEAM PLAYER, FROM BULLPEN CATCHER TO TEAM MANAGER TO SCOREKEEPER. ANY OF THEM WOULD ALLOW HIM TO BE A PART OF THE TEAM EVERYDAY!

To: CoachLisle@CoachLisle.com
From: coach@iamtherealmvp.com
Subject: This Year's Tee-Ball MVP Goes To...

Dear Coach Lisle,

I coach tee-ball in our local rec league consisting of 4-6 year-old boys. I have been coaching for a long time and was coaching my youngest son's team.

Last month at our end-of-the-season party, we handed out trophies to all the kids and told some funny stories about the season. Everyone was having a great time until one of the dad's stood up and presented his son an MVP trophy that he had custom made. I had to spend the next 2 days responding to other parents' emails who were confused as to why we handed out an MVP trophy to a six-year-old.

Sincerely,
Not Amused

To: CoachLisle@CoachLisle.com
From: hawaiianshirtcoach@geemail.com
Subject: Trademark Infringement

Dear Coach Lisle,

The email below is from a 10-U softball parent who did not take it well when I suggested to the team that, in lieu of tie-dying our uniforms at an upcoming Saturday pool party, we instead try to make them look like Hawaiian Shirts by painting palm trees on them. I also promised the coaches would wear matching Hawaiian shirts at our next tournament.

Dear Coach,

On the way home from practice Tina repeated to me what you said about the fact that you and the other coaches were going to wear Hawaiian shirts at the next tournament.

I actually waited 24 hours (cool down time) to address your vile comments made in front of my daughter. I love this league and all of the relationships our family has built in the name of GOOD sportsmanship and I'm questioning how your comment, again in front of my daughter, aligns with the league's ideal of fostering good moral fiber in sports. As for the shirts, I'm a top realtor in North Florida and the Hawaiian shirts that I wear are my TRADEMARK look.

My wife heard from Tina what you said, not from me (I down played it) and she wanted Tina off your team. It's good that you take time to coach, but if I hear any crap come from your mouth in the presence of those girls again I'm going to be all over it. I will be speaking to the league about this incident. "Loose lips sink ships." You may be too young to have heard that. It means be careful of what comes out of your mouth, it might hurt someone... a lot.

Sincerely,

Trademark Dad

DALE STEVENSON

REALTOR

The HAWAIIAN SHIRT GUY! ™

NORTH FLORIDA'S TOP REALTOR *

* AMONG REALTORS WHO WEAR HAWAIIAN SHIRTS

To: CoachLisle@CoachLisle.com
From: coach@theseparentsthough.org
Subject: Cross Lacrosse Dad

Dear Coach Lisle,

I am a high school lacrosse coach. Last season, I had a dad come up to me and start yelling at me about why his son was not playing over others. In this particular instance, we were playing a lesser opponent and I was giving some other players some playing time. It was literally the only game his son had not started all year, and it was the FIRST game his father had come to (nearly fifteen games into the season).

The player's father proceeded to rip the jersey off the kid's back, handed it in for him, and they both walked off. After about fifteen minutes of me getting my ears chewed out, the player came back, told me that he was sorry, and that he told his father leave.

Needless to say, this kid was one of our key defenders and finished out the rest of the season as one of our best overall players.

Sincerely,
At Least It Ended Well

To: CoachLisle@CoachLisle.com
From: mrssmith@geemail.com
Subject: Roster "Adjustment"

Dear Coach Lisle,

My son was playing 11U boys' soccer and has been playing in this organization for a few years now. It has been a great team in recent seasons, led by conscientious coaches and an active but demanding manager.

There have predictably been a lot of changes in the roster from season to season. The boys are young and at this age we still get kids who are brand new to soccer, or who play only one season of soccer each year.

Which brings me to this season, when this particular team got switched around a bit and new players were added to their roster.

The head coach - very likeable and respected - and his manager/wife, were trying to "adjust" the roster for the upcoming season, to get rid of the players they didn't want.

Our team used an online program for parents to click on what games/practices their kids were available for and which ones they weren't (vacations, etc.). The coaches decided that in order to get rid of the kids they didn't want, they would go into the Availability tab and change some of the boys' attendance from "yes" to "no." They then went to the head of the club and complained that these boys were never at practices and games, even though they were.

The parents who were affected by the status changes went to the board and there was a full investigation that concluded in the culpability of the coach and his wife/manager. This has resulted in the head coach being demoted to assistant, and his manager/wife losing her position. People are shocked that this likeable couple could be so underhanded.

Sincerely,
Mrs. Smith

COACH LISLE'S COMMENTARY

NOTHING "SHOCKS" ME ANYMORE WHEN IT COMES TO THE LENGTHS THAT PEOPLE WILL GO TO GET WHAT THEY WANT. HAVING SAID THAT, WHAT MAKES THIS STORY SOMETHING MORE THAN SHOCKING IS THAT THIS HAPPENED IN 11U SOCCER. 11U SHOULD BE ABOUT DEVELOPMENT AND FUN; NOT JUST WINNING.

DON'T GET ME WRONG, I THINK WINNING AND COMPETITION ARE GREAT! BUT THEY AREN'T THE THINGS THAT MATTER MOST FOR KIDS THIS AGE. IF YOU'RE LOOKING FOR A TRAVEL BALL TEAM OR ORGANIZATION IN ANY SPORT, I HIGHLY ENCOURAGE YOU TO LOOK FOR COACHES WHO ARE NOT ONLY FOCUSED ON DEVELOPMENT BUT WHO ARE ALSO HAVING FUN COACHING.

WHICH LEADS ME TO A THOUGHT I HAVE ABOUT THIS STORY. WHY DIDN'T THE ORGANIZATION SHOW THIS COACH THE DOOR? HE DELIBERATELY SABOTAGED ATHLETES WITH THE INTENT OF ELIMINATING THEM FROM THEIR PROGRAM. IN MY OPINION, DEMOTION ISN'T STRONG ENOUGH. HE SHOULDN'T BE ALLOWED TO BE A COACH; NOT EVEN AS AN ASSISTANT!

THE ORGANIZATION HAD AN OPPORTUNITY TO SUPPORT ATHLETES (10 AND 11 YEAR OLD KIDS, REMEMBER) AND THEIR FAMILIES BY SENDING A MESSAGE THAT THEY WOULDN'T TOLERATE MANIPULATION AND DECEPTION FROM AN ADULT.

To: CoachLisle@CoachLisle.com
From: foulmouthedcoach@yawhew.com
Subject: This Email Sucks

Dear Coach Lisle,

We always jokingly tell our 9-10 year olds to have fun and "don't suck." I got it from Chicago Cubs manager Joe Maddon who taught the Cubs to "embrace the suck." And Cubs players wore shirts the year they won the World Series that said "Try Not To Suck" on them.

Because the kids had embraced the saying all season, we decided to put it on the sleeve of a jersey, in small font, and the kids loved it. Except one new kid whose parents didn't like the phrase.

Dear Coach,

I wanted to make you aware of an issue that I have so we can maintain clear and bilateral communications. Upon arriving home late last night I was pleased to find the beautiful selection of caps and team jerseys displayed on the back of our living room couch. However, upon close inspection I find the phrase "Don't Suck" emblazoned on the left sleeve of one of the shirts. I want you to understand that I could hardly be more delighted to find one of the very words that Chris has recently been in a mild amount of trouble for generously overusing right there on his sleeve! Can you imagine my jubilance?

Clearly, I have very little wiggle room in admonishing anyone's choice of words. Please don't think that I am trying to come off as superior or pious. I have an awful use of "adult" vocabulary and I am frequently reminded that "little ears" need not be indoctrinated to colorful speech. I also don't put it on a shirt. Not everything that is said in the locker room or dugout needs to be repeated for all ears or scripted on a shirt. I generally appreciate the gesture but take exception with the choice to print on the uniform.

Regards,
Dan

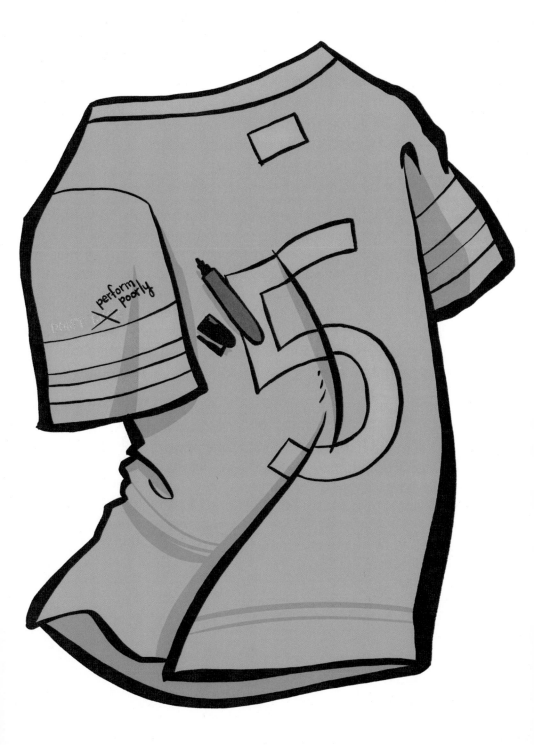

To: DearCoach@CoachLisle.com
From: upsetparent@yawhew.com
Subject: Rec League Birther

Dear Tournament Director,

Last weekend my daughter's 8U All-Star team paid and played in your "All Star Rec Tournament." However, the only team we lost to was Concord's "All Star" team which we later found out was really a travel team. We also found out from players on the team that they were "about to turn 11 next month."

I have no problem losing fair and square, but having an 8-year-old rec team compete against a travel team with girls that were as big as I am is counterproductive and completely unfair. The "All Star" team coaches felt that it was appropriate to run up the score to an almost 20 point spread. Our coaches called them out and said it was unsportsmanlike, and their coaches proceeded to yell, "Why don't you get us out?" I cannot tell you how offended I was by the conduct of these coaches and the parents. If you are going to invite us to a rec tournament, it damn sure *should* be!

If this team plans to participate in any future tournaments that we enter, I will let that league know about our experience with this team and I will demand birth certificates for any players that they enter. We are all out here to have fun and win, but, most importantly, to teach girls how to work as a team and show good sportsmanship. That All Star team made that difficult for us to do that with our girls. I hope you take this into consideration because most every parent that I talked to or overheard from our team or opposing teams felt the same way that I do.

Sincerely,
Show Us The Birth Certificates

Tournament Director's Note: This "All-Star" team was comprised of the same age girls (8 year olds) no one on their team was even close to 11 years old.

To: CoachLisle@CoachLisle.com
From: flabbergasted@yawhew.com
Subject: Not Seeing Eye To Eye

Dear Coach Lisle,

A few years go, I was coaching a 12U softball team with twelve girls on the team. After our final game of the season in which we lost, I had a dad come up to me as I was leaving the field and started yelling at me that I ruined softball for his daughter. He said she sat on the bench more than any other player, was always at the bottom of the lineup, had far fewer at bats, and she played left field too often. That was his impression of the season. He saved it all up for the very end. He never approached me once throughout the season to say he had concerns.

I was flabbergasted of course. Not only because I was completely blindsided, but because I took great pains every week to set up my batting lineups and fielding positions for every game ahead of time in a spreadsheet. In doing so, I made certain that every player sat equal times and kept track throughout the season. I moved people around in the batting lineup, but I did use a couple of more consistent hitters in the top of the lineup. Because I did all of this on my computer — and because I had all of our game sheets — I was able to show him with 100% confidence that his daughter's number of at bats almost exactly matched the team average, that all players had sat out the same number of innings, and that his daughter's fielding positions were split equally between infield and outfield assignments. Moreover, his daughter came out to every practice with a smile and a great work ethic, she participated fully, and interacted well with all teammates and coaches. She never complained or frowned all summer long. Everything pointed to her having had a great season on my team. In spite of my irrefutable evidence to the contrary, her dad insisted I was wrong and had made up data to protect myself! I very nearly walked away from coaching that year!

Cheers,
Greg

COACH LISLE'S COMMENTARY

FIRST OF ALL, I LOVE THAT THIS COACH CREATED A SPREADSHEET AND TRACKED THE LINEUPS AND PLAYING TIME THROUGHOUT THE SEASON! IT'S A GREAT WAY TO ENSURE FAIRNESS AND OPPORTUNITY TO ATHLETES AT THE YOUNGER LEVEL, REGARDLESS OF TALENT.

PARENTS AND COACHES SEEING THINGS THROUGH DIFFERENT LENSES IS A REGULAR OCCURRENCE. SO COULD THE FATHER'S OUTBURST BE AVOIDED? MAYBE. MAYBE NOT. WHAT CAN I SAY FOR SURE IS THAT IF THERE IS A LESSON TO BE LEARNED FOR COACHES IT IS THIS:

ALWAYS OVER COMMUNICATE.

I TELL PARENTS MY PLAN AND THEN DO MY BEST TO EXPLAIN WHY I MADE IT. THEN, WHEN THE OPPORTUNITY PRESENTS ITSELF, I'LL EXPLAIN IT ALL OVER AGAIN. IT'S POSSIBLE THIS COACH ASSUMED PARENTS AND PLAYERS WOULD NOTICE HIS PLAN AS IT PLAYED OUT, AND THIS FATHER AND DAUGHTER DIDN'T PICK UP ON IT.

To: CoachLisle@CoachLisle.com
From: coach@justryingtodomyjob.org
Subject: Dad Coach < Actual Coach

Dear Coach Lisle,

I have been coaching high school softball for over 25 years. I began coaching at a pretty young age (25). In only my second year of coaching, I had a moment I've never forgotten about.

In the middle of a game, with me standing a few feet away, a dad summoned his daughter and said very loudly, "Don't look at your coaches or listen to them. You look at me and listen to me".

As a young coach who was intimidated by this father, I didn't say anything in response or address it later. All season long, his daughter would look at him from the batter's box and the field for instructions.

I never made that mistake again.

Sincerely,
Don't Let The Dads Get Ya Down

To: CoachLisle@CoachLisle.com
From: assistant@igotyourbackcoach.org
Subject: Respect Your Elders

Dear Coach Lisle,

A couple of years ago, I was an assistant high school girls volleyball coach. Prior to a game, one of our starters was being very rude and hateful towards the head coach. The head coach proceeded to not start her. As soon as her mother realized her daughter wasn't starting she came storming down from the bleachers. She yelled at the head coach, "Why is she not playing?!" My head coach replied calmly, "Because she was being rude and hateful to me."

The mom became irate and said, "I'm not gonna keep taking off work to come to these games and not see her play!"

I then turned to the mother and said, "I would be mad, too, if I took off work and my kid was being rude to grown folks. It sounds like you need to speak with your child about that."

The mother grumbled under her breath but returned to the bleachers where she sat quietly for most of the match.

Sincerely,
Solid Burn

To: coachlisle@gmail.com
From: whathavelgottenmyselfinto@yawhew.com
Subject: How NOT To Coach Eight-Year-Olds

Dear Coach Lisle,

Just a few weeks ago, at our 8u practice, I was coming from work and was going to be about 10 minutes late. I reached out to all the parents and one dad volunteered to get them warmed up.

When I arrive, I walk up to the field to find this dad with his shirt off, cigarette hanging from his lip, beer in one hand bat in the other and two more beers stacked on home plate as he was hitting them grounders!

Needless to say I had to have a dos and don'ts conversation with him that I still don't think he understood.

Sincerely,
What Have I Gotten Myself Into

To: CoachLisle@CoachLisle.com
From: overreactingdadsaretheworst@yawhew.com
Subject: Nominee For "Worst Dad Ever"

Dear Coach Lisle,

I wanted to share what happened in our 12U baseball game last month.

We were down by one run, bases loaded with two outs and the batter had a 3-0 count. I called time out and told the kid not to swing until he had one strike.

The very next pitch came in at the hitter's eyes. He decided to swing at ball four, popped the ball up to the pitcher, and we lost. As I walked off the field, I noticed a father had swung open the gate and was running at me at full speed. He was screaming and cursing that he was going to knock me out because he thought I had instructed the kid to swing. As he charged closer, the wet grass caused him to slip and fall. The fall seemed to knock some sense into him. He got up quietly and walked away.

A few weeks later, this same father's son was pitching. He was having a bad inning. He gave up a couple runs and had a couple walks, but got out of the inning. The next inning, his son walked the first batter. The father ran onto the field, grabbed his son by the shirt, and slapped him across the face. He then dragged him off the field to the car and drove off.

I reported all this to the league and I haven't seen the parent or the kid since.

Sincerely,
I Hope That Kid Is OK

COACH LISLE'S COMMENTARY

FOR THE MOST PART, I LIKE THE WAY THIS COACH HANDLED THIS SITUATION. HOWEVER, I THINK THE COACH HAD AN OPPORTUNITY TO STEP INTO WHAT SEEMS LIKE A TOXIC SITUATION WITH THIS FATHER AND SON. AND THAT'S BIGGER THAN BASEBALL.

IT SOUNDS LIKE THIS DAD COULD USE SOME HELP. MAYBE HE WOULDN'T HEAR IT FROM THIS COACH, BUT IT'S WORTH A SHOT. IT'S DEFINITELY WORTH IT FOR THAT KID. JUST BECAUSE THE FATHER AND SON LEFT THE LEAGUE DOESN'T MEAN THAT TOXIC BEHAVIOR WILL CHANGE.

IT'S FAR MORE LIKELY THAT THIS DAD WILL RUIN THE SPORT OF BASEBALL FOR HIS SON. IT'S ALSO POSSIBLE THAT THIS FATHER/SON RELATIONSHIP COULD BE DAMAGED UNLESS SOMEONE INTERVENES. AND I GET IT; SOMETIMES IT SEEMS LIKE "IT'S JUST BASEBALL." BUT IT NEVER IS.

IT'S ABOUT BEING A KID TRYING TO GROW UP AND BEING A PARENT TRYING TO HELP OUR KIDS BECOME ADULTS. COACHES GET TO PLAY A PART IN THAT STORY. THAT'S A HUGE RESPONSIBILITY. IT'S ALSO A PRIVILEGE AND A GIFT.

ACKNOWLEDGEMENTS

I'd like to first and foremost thank my dad, this book has been his idea for many years now and I only executed on it.

Thank you to Justin McRoberts, for shepherding this project from concept to completion, taking a set of stories and emails and helping me weave them together so that the reader could immerse themselves in a story.

Wes Molebash who did the incredible illustrations in this book. I'm so glad to have met him and can't wait to do more projects with him.

Huge thanks go out to the folks who have supported my work over the years. Social Media Followers, Coaches, Parents, Players, folks who came to my camps and clinics across the country and the members of The Hitting Vault — y'all are the reason any of this happens.

To "The Thread": I wouldn't be where I am without you guys. Glad to be living life with you all. HMB, RBN, Mona Lisa, CSB, and WOC.

And finally, I'd like to thank my wife for always supporting me in this career path and holding our family together all these years. If she ever had the time, I know her book of coaching wives stories would be a best-seller as well.

THE BASE FOUNDATION

All of the proceeds from this book's sales will be donated to *The BASE* organization. Founded in 2013 by Robert Lewis, Jr., *The BASE* operates a premier national urban youth academy that combines sports and academic opportunities through a methodology that cultivates excellence, belief and love.

The BASE model plays a key role in shifting the national mindset and re-imagining pathways to success for urban youth.

The BASE has served over 8,000 boys and girls on more than 600 teams, competing not only locally but also nationally and internationally — from Florida, Virginia, Nevada, and Chicago to Japan and the Dominican Republic.

To learn more visit **www.TheBase.org**

 **MATT LISLE** is a husband, father, and coach. He has coached at every single level of athletics from Little League to MLB and currently serves as the Hitting Analytics Instructor for MLB's Chicago White Sox. A father of five and grandfather of two, Lisle has been involved in youth athletics as both a player, coach, and parent for over 35 years and shares his experience and advice on social media with the handle @CoachLisle as well as his website CoachLisle.com.

He lives in the San Francisco Bay Area with his wife Jessica, five children Alicia, Chappie, Chase, Presley, Crosby, and their 150 pound English Mastiff, Winston (The Beast).